It's Easier to Dance:

Living Beyond Boundaries

A Memoir by:

Annie Laurie Harris, M.Ed.

It's Easier to Dance

Annie Laurie Harris

It's Easier to Dance

For information Email:
Poetry.cardsusa@gmail.com:

Published in the United States of America

Acknowledgements

I am indebted to so many for encouraging me in this revision of my book that it is impossible to name all of them. However, I must name a few who continue to support me without reservation.

My family who allowed me to go my own way even though they worried how I would manage.

Thank you to Jeremy Frank and Ann McLaren—your friendship,, encouragement and gentle, yet probing questions allowed me to complete the final and most difficult chapter.

Thank you to Stephanie Zonar of the Penn State Lady Lion Basketball staff for editing this revised edition.

Table of Contents

Foreword

All except the last chapter of this book is written in retrospect, mostly from my own memories, what family members told me over the years and what I wrote in my journals beginning around age 12. I did not grow up in public and there is still so much I don't know about living in society.

Therefore, I am not politically correct (I keep trying) in my self-expression, having never learned the rules that the able-bodied learn in daily interactions with peers and those in authority or higher socioeconomic status. I wrote this book according to the period of history I'm talking about. I do not mean to offend anyone but do think it's important to speak authentically. I hope you will hear, see and feel what I felt as an African-American child, teenager and woman with a complex developmental disability in a world where the decision-making power lay in the hands of white able-bodied men. I'm speaking about institutional, systemic bias, not personal preference. There may be some overlap.

Introduction

If a memoir is a window into someone's life, then clearly there are many windows into which we never see. This leaves us to make assumptions about who lives in the house we call the human body.

It's Easier to Dance is the story of Annie Laurie Harris, an African American woman born with cerebral palsy. Every chapter is an interesting and compelling story that begins with the circumstances of her birth in the late-1940s. She traversed challenging terrain before the advent of the civil rights movement, the feminist movement and the Americans with Disabilities Act (ADA) as we know it. As she tells her own story, she also reveals the unfolding evolution of social awareness over six decades into the 21st century.

As the first chapter begins, it becomes clear that this is a complex individual who is shaped by all of her experiences, several of which are directly associated with her physical attributes while others are a direct result of her single-minded positive belief in her own success and potential. Her personality is unique and she offers insights that are rarely shared. She describes a life lived in defiance of ongoing social stereotypes and barriers, and with joyous completion of several remarkable achievements such as a graduate degree, international travel and living independently. It's Easier to Dance encourages all of us to speak in our own voice, and to believe those who speak for themselves.

Harris addresses issues of equity, education, sex, relationship building, life changing acts of kindness, belief in the supernatural and the power of love. Each of these topics are candidly covered through her experiences. Her story is told in a very human voice that commands light upon things that are otherwise hidden in shadows and disguised in the name of the public good.

While race and gender are predisposed, unchanging conditions of specific groups, disability can happen to anyone. The preconceived notions of society are not solely based on singular traits, but on the combination of one's attributes. Many of Harris' experiences are directly related to being African American, being a woman and having cerebral palsy. Many situations might have ended differently were she only one or two of the three. And then, her personality and disposition are woven throughout the mix, dictating the strategies she chose to manage her life.

It's Easier to Dance addresses a single question repeatedly: How can individuals be encouraged to look past physical trappings to see the wonderful attributes of each other? Annie Laure Harris helps us to see ourselves.

Having interacted with Ms. Harris on several occasions over many years, her choice to continue living independently has rendered her a local public figure with all the advantages and challenges that this brings. Though some may not know her name, she is typically recognized by combination of her race, gender, physical attributes, mechanical assistance, and vibrant personality.

Annie Harris is an activist with little patience for hypocrites and inconsistency. Her life has been fraught with incredible barriers to climb, many placed there deliberately as an impassible test designed to prove the worthlessness of trying- yet she overcame each of them defying the odds again and again.

At 60 years old, she is the oldest known African American woman with cerebral palsy to be living independently. This memoir is a rare gift. Her story informs us of the humanity we all share. It provides a personalized history that encourages us all to contribute to a more caring, accepting society.

Amy Freeman, Ph.D.
Assistant Dean of Engineering Diversity
The Pennsylvania State University

Living Beyond Boundaries

Chapter 1

My First Advocate and Teacher

Imagine going through life in slow motion. Falling, getting up and falling again—more times than one could ever want to count or remember. The next 24 hours would dawn and I'd begin again: falling, getting up…until the day came that I didn't fall as often and I knew I could make it.

After twenty-six hours of labor, Louise Harris, a forty-year-old woman with medium brown skin gave birth to a 10 pound baby girl. She had an eighth grade education having she was forced to quit school to care for her siblings. She was married to a man of equal education and had six other children.

I have always been told—with little variation—that after my birth the doctor went into my mother's room and told her I had been born dead. Instead of being upset, my understanding is that my mother looked at her family doctor, who knew her well, and said, "My baby could not be dead because I told God that if I had to have another baby, I wanted a girl."

So she told him to work on her baby girl while she prayed. Sometime later the doctor returned and said that he had gotten the baby breathing, but there was no sucking reflex, and he did not hold out hope for her daughter's survival. This was the first of many medical prognoses that I would defy.

I remained in the hospital for three months. My parents and older siblings were allowed to look at me through glass every few hours and did so around the clock until they could take me home. Around the age of 15 months, I still could not sit up independently and made no attempt to walk. I was diagnosed with cerebral palsy and the medical prognosis was very bleak.

They told my mother that I would need to be institutionalized and would not live to see adulthood. They said I would never be able to live independently, attend school or do any of the activities that were characteristic of "normal" children. A stubborn woman, my mother rejected the prognosis and the opinions of the doctors. She insisted that she would treat me like all her other children, and raise me in the same way.

Just as she treated me the same when it came to getting an education, she also insisted that I learn appropriate behaviors that would allow be to establish habits that would lead to a standard of living that would be viewed as successful by society. Although she was told by many professionals that holding me to able bodied standards was unrealistic, her Christian faith, and values sustained her. Her relentless advocacy on my behalf frustrated the medical doctors at the time as she refused to give permission to surgically cut my hamstrings, a common surgery done around age 12 which prevents appropriate growth and ensures that some with cerebral palsy will not continue to be able to bear weight appropriately as an adult She also did not insist that I take the prescribed medication that causes a shaking of the head and adds to the misdiagnosis of an intellectual deficit not present in my situation.

This deep religious belief still found in religious traditions that believe in a loving image of God, remains in the the African American Christian church. Though it was believed by some, that having a child with such complex disabilities was a "punishment" from God. My mother, siblings, and extended family did not hold to this misinterpretation that was not part of the belief system of Africans. I recall the ritual of naming a child from the movie, "roots". The words, "Behold the only thing greater than yourself" are incanted as the, infant is lifted toward the heavens.

Oddly enough, this belief that my life was a gift from God was the deciding factor in my <u>not</u> being placed in an institution. As good Christian woman, my mother chose to view her child with cerebral palsy as part of her family along with her other children ." **Any** distortion and misunderstanding that her baby's disability was a "punishment" from God was unacceptable to my family, although many in the Judeo Christian Tradition still ascribe to this misinterpretation of some scripture passages if out of context..

In my 40's I began to realize the depth of her sacrificial love for me. I started to cherish her memory and the sacrifices she made so that I could grow into an adult and know how to take care of myself in a world that still makes it a VERY difficult!. If I had been raised according to the time period in which I was born I would not be living the independent lifestyle I live today. Therefore, my gratitude for her life is as deep as her maternal love was for me.

At the age of seven years, I started school. She soon told me to quit using the word "can't." She told me just not to use it anymore and I listened. Even as an adult I rarely say, "I can't," except that I can't run. By high school things became more challenging and people began to wonder about my future.

In 1966, I got a new teacher, Janie Griffith. She had just graduated from Slippery Rock College with a degree in Special Education. It took her only a few weeks to notice my advanced intelligence and she began to inquire how I could get a public high school diploma while attending the special school for crippled children. Hickory High School was only a few doors down from my school. They made arrangements to bring the state required high school courses to me via programmed learning materials and my physical therapist, Jerome Wandel, taught me biology. During this first of many turning points in my education, my mother took a very active role in the Parent Teachers Association.

In June 1968, I graduated from Hickory High School. My mother had a big open house for me and everybody came to celebrate. Mrs. Thompson, LPN at the Mercer County Crippled Children's School and responsible for all students' personal care, loved me for 12 years like her own child. She had a difficult time letting me go. She bought me a jewelry box full of useable items, one being a button hook that would allow me to button blouses, skirts, etc., something that I couldn't do before.

The only thing more compelling than my mother's insistence that I be educated was that I learn how to take care of my personal hygiene needs, dress like a female and be perceived as attractive in the world. On school days she would help me get ready. On the weekends, however, I had to do everything independently. It took around four hours to wash, dress and tie my orthopedic shoes in the morning. My mother had a rule that we couldn't go downstairs in our bathrobes, so I had to be fully dressed before I ate breakfast.

I was always chosen for whatever publicity that was needed by my special school. One year I was the poster child for the United Cerebral Palsy Association. Whenever someone wanted to write an article about my school, I was the one chosen to be photographed. That was part of my privileged status that I once took for granted.

In my first years of school, everyone recognized my above average intelligence, but could not imagine how I would ever develop the skills to live independently in society or work at a job. The involuntary motions and drooling were seen as the aspects of having cerebral palsy that would carry the highest social stigma and would prevent me from living as the able-bodied of equal intelligence. The addition of having a significant speech impediment gave validity to the opinions that any resemblance to a "normal" life was outside the realm of possibility. People saw these major obstacles as seemingly impossible to overcome.

Chapter 2

Ticket to Freedom

My mother always stressed the great importance of education. From early in my childhood, she insisted that I go to school like any other child. She became my first teacher. But college wasn't considered a possibility.

After getting my high school diploma, I went to a rehabilitation center to enter a typing program. No one bothered to tell me that in order to be a clerk typist, you needed to be able to type at least 40 wpm with a maximum of five errors. When I learned this, I felt betrayed and quit the program, returning home depressed.

I wouldn't see my vocational rehabilitation counselor because he wanted me to go to a sheltered workshop for those with the primary diagnosis of "mental retardation." I didn't get dressed or eat regularly. I wondered what would happen to me.

Finally, my brother, a graduate student at Penn State, asked one of his professors if there was some way that his younger sister could go to college. The professor had influence, and recommended to the appropriate people that the university grant me permission to attend a branch campus for 2 terms and then base my acceptance on my GPA.

In September 1972 (the year congress passed the Right to Education Law which allowed children with significant disabilities to attend public schools) I became an adjunct student at the Penn State Shenango Valley campus. I made the Dean's List and that next fall I began my undergraduate degree at this campus.

Older than the typical undergraduate, I made friends among the young instructors, who loved having me in their classes. My academic advisor recommended an exemption from the language (something I later regretted) or the undergraduate speech requirement, which included giving public speeches. I talked to the instructor, James Elder, who said "Annie, you have important things to say to the world so you might as well start in my class." Except for statistics, college was not particularly intellectually challenging.

When my transfer to the main campus became imminent, the huge problem of mobility presented itself. The vocational rehabilitation system, designed to assist physically disabled veterans back to work, was introduced by the United States federal government around the end of WWII. At this point in history, those with physical disabilities were not actually integrated into public schools, much less institutions of higher education.

A staff member with the Vocational

Rehabilitation Office, dark-haired, 6'4"
Mark Funkhouser, didn't subscribe to the
typical vocational rehabilitation system
mentality. He told his supervisor (my
rehabilitation counselor) that I needed "an
Amigo"—the first electric scooter (no
treads on the tires, acid batteries, and no
brakes!). Mark, by the way, drove a white
Volkswagen Bug and the first time I saw
him get out of it, I thought he was going to
keep going up!

In the spring of 1973, the Rehabilitation
Act passed, requiring preference be given
to those with severe disabilities, even
though they were the most difficult to
employ. This uncompromising novice to
the rehabilitation state government
bureaucracy was persuasive in getting me
the scooter. He accused his supervisor of
not wanting me to succeed, but only
wanting to obey the recent amendment to
the 1973 Rehabilitation Act that mandated
priority consideration for the most severely
impaired.

The summer of 1974 I transferred to the University Park campus. The influential professor set me up in McKee Hall, close to my classes. He guaranteed one of his students a "C" in his class, if he would help me get around campus. I'll never forget Greg, with curly blond hair and blue eyes. He encouraged me to explore the speed of my scooter and I still have the scars! Back then there were no curb cuts, but it came with a portable ramp. Another student was offered the same deal, and he helped me with my evening meal. He'd been in the Peace Corp, had a hot plate and could cook anything. I even had a toaster oven in my room for breakfast.

Academics still didn't prove much of a challenge, even at the main campus. Mostly I enjoyed the interaction and opportunity to learn and socialize with other people. To get class notes, I carried around a piece of carbon paper and asked whoever sat beside me to put it in their notebook. My nearly photographic memory made it easy to pass mid-term and final exams. Soon I began

receiving honorary academic awards.
In 1975 *Essence Magazine,* a publication primarily by and for African American women, selected me as one of 12 black women at American universities most likely to succeed and emerge as a leader. I remember someone recognizing me in Chicago's O'Hare Airport as I was traveling to see my sister that summer.

During those undergraduate years at University Park I started to have a social life. At 25 years old, I dated for the first time. There were so many social rules I didn't know, having grown up without a peer group and/or age appropriate social relationships. I felt (and often still feel) "out of place" socially with people my own chronological age. After a certain number of years, I am convinced that age is irrelevant, Therefore, I preferred to socialize with those I felt most comfortable with as I do now..

I graduated with distinction from the highly respected Pennsylvania State University on March 3, 1976. My entire family, the Anglican Priest who had baptized me three years previously and my two best friends from college came to my graduation. My beautician, Loretta Wilson, and her husband hosted an open house in my honor following the ceremony. That day represented a monumental accomplishment in my life!

I had established a routine that went relatively smoothly until it came time to apply for jobs. The same people who supported my academic pursuits suddenly quit speaking to me. The professor who had used his influence to get me into school, did not believe I could or should work with people, recommending that I work in a library where I would not be seen publicly on a daily basis.

I was hurt, disappointed, confused and angry. From the very beginning, I had told people that I wanted my college degree more than anything in the world and was determined to do whatever necessary to get it. They just didn't believe me. A degree was my ticket out of the stereotypical lifestyle presumed because of my developmental disability and perhaps my bicultural background. Education provided a huge stepping stone to an independent life, and the working world.

I worked full-time at the Easter Seal Society of Centre and Clinton Counties and United Cerebral Palsy of Central Pennsylvania. Both agencies provided services to people with a wide variety of disabilities. I soon discovered that I did not enjoy working with those who had the same issues that I had dealt with all my life. People presumed that I not only wanted to, but should work with those with similar disabilities. I felt stereotyped into "playing" a role that didn't "fit" my interests or intellectual capacity, so I chose a different direction.

I continued living in State College, PA, determined to earn an income that would supplement my monthly disability check.

After seeking the advice of several friends, I thought of turning my hobby of writing poetry into a small business called Poetry Cards. A friend from my church volunteered to illustrate and write the calligraphy for six cards to get me started. Following those initial designs, I paid several artists a flat fee to illustrate my poems and write them in artistic calligraphy. For the next 8 years I created, marketed, distributed and sold my own greeting cards to wholesale and retail buyers. During these years I also traveled, taking my work with me. I frequently visited friends in Allentown, PA, and explored the New England coastline of Maine, where a close friend lived.

At each destination, I established an outlet for my poetry cards to ensure a return trip. People welcomed and invited me to write at their homes, once they discovered that I loved being by the ocean. When people asked "what do you do?", I replied "I'm an artist, I write poetry." Their responses amazed me. They didn't seem to care how much money I made, or if I made any at all. It was a "status symbol" to say I was an artist or a poet. I never had that before. Still, it wasn't the intellectual challenge I craved and it did not provide the opportunity to use my intellect to its full potential. I wanted something more…a professional identity.

Chapter 3

The World of Work

I didn't begin to develop a professional identity—a sense of who I was in the world of work—until graduate school. I had always thought about securing and keeping a job (especially given my limitations), but not about how others would view the kind of work I did, regardless of the position I held.

This professional identity began to emerge at the end of my first year of graduate school in 1984, when I was doing a practicum in preparation for an internship as a counselor in an inpatient facility for men dealing with chemical dependency. I had been offered a full scholarship to graduate school at my alma mater if I majored in rehabilitation. Since I had not enjoyed working with people who had similar disabilities to my own, I was intrigued when a young man presented with symptoms that my supervisor recognized as alcoholism. As a recovering alcoholic, he knew that this young man's problems showed a pattern of alcohol consumption indicative of alcoholism. This surprised me and I wanted to know more. Aware of the prevalence of alcohol abuse in our society, I wanted to know how to recognize it. My supervisor was in the process of establishing Talleyrand Retreat, an inpatient facility for adult males. I asked if I could intern there and enjoyed the work immensely. It quickly became my expertise and I was given increasingly more responsibility during my internship.

Before graduation, they hired me full-time to supervise clients with multiple diagnoses as well as undergraduate and graduate interns. I became particularly astute at the initial diagnostic evaluations and intake interviews. I especially enjoyed the teaching aspect of supervising interns and soon developed a reputation of being "hard but good." I was particularly interested in helping interns establish appropriate boundaries while interacting with the clients in a therapeutic environment. In addition, I became a clinician in the director's private practice, seeing clients on an outpatient basis, as well as maintaining my responsibilities as a counselor in the inpatient setting.

With funding cuts, I was laid off in the fall of 1986. At the same time, my friend in Boston had an opening for a housemate and agreed that I could move in as long as I agreed to assume complete responsibility for taking care of myself. On January 7, 1987 I moved to Arlington, MA, a suburb of Boston. Within four months I interviewed for a job as a clinician at Habit Management, the first private for profit methadone clinic in the Commonwealth of Massachusetts.

When they asked if I needed any special accommodations, I requested double vacation and sick time so that I would not become over-extended physically from working full time. They agreed to this. When I asked, however, to come in late on Tuesdays so that I could attend yoga class, they raised their eyebrows. I asked, "If I said it was physical therapy, would you have a problem?"

They said, "No."

"Well, it's not physical therapy" I said, "but yoga is the discipline I use to maintain my strength and stamina."

I asked for one more concession, to have no more than 30 clients on my caseload (half of my able-bodied colleagues' load) in exchange for as many intakes as they wanted me to do.

When they asked why they should accommodate me when they could hire somebody else who would not require such consideration, I looked the clinical director in the eye and said, "I'm the best, look at me, I have to be among the best." He smiled and nodded in agreement. Then he asked me to meet with a group of men who had been in recovery at least 5 years. He just wanted to know how they would feel about someone with my disability being their counselor. I thought it was a fair request.

We met and I told them about my life, education and view of addiction as just another disability—not all that different than other complex disabilities. After asking quite a few questions, they looked at the director and simply said, "Hire her." And so he did.

They recognized me as a professional woman with or without a disability. The widely held assumption that one is more professionally qualified to work with a specific population due to having the same or similar disability is an inaccurate presumption and a major contributor to the discrepancies in employment, education and income level of people with disabilities compared to their able-bodied peers. Everyone pays a high price in limiting the level of education and career options for those with complex developmental or congenital disabilities. The consequences for such bias may limit a brilliant mind from pursuing a degree in something totally unrelated to disabilities.

The therapeutic population in the city was different than what I was used to. The primary drugs abused were heroin and cocaine. I observed many more legal issues, physical illnesses and a variety of lifestyles that challenged my personal belief system, stereotype images and beliefs about those addicted to "hard" drugs. I evaluated physicians, attorneys, lab technicians and prostitutes for treatment.

As a result, I developed an ability to work with a culturally diverse population with a wide variety of lifestyles, income levels and social status, not to mention abilities and limitations. My skills earned me the reputation of being able to evaluate and correctly refer clients to appropriate service providers for their needs. These complex, multi-faceted situations taught me to zero in on a particular problem, while treating a client as a whole person. I saw myself as an advocate and educator, rather than therapist and counselor. This professional identity, once established, carried over to either a volunteer or paid position. Defining myself by my professional identity helped me to maintain a healthy self-worth in a society where work dominates one's validity. This dispels being viewed as an invalid despite having cerebral palsy, a physical disability that continues to challenge me to live courageously and create opportunities in every area of my life.

It's Easier To Dance

Chapter 4

A Change in Identity

Until the age of forty, I defined myself in terms of my physical disability—cerebral palsy, a neurological developmental disability typically occurring in utero or during the birthing process that can affect any area of the brain. In my case, athetoid is characterized by involuntary gross motor movement, muscle spasticity, and speech impairment. No intellectual impairment was found, however, it was presumed because of my lack of ability to articulate words. I believed myself to have more in common with disabled and white people than "colored" people. This view of myself changed significant as will be described in the next chapter.

I moved to the San Francisco Bay Area in March, 1989. having been recruited by The

World Institute on Disability (WID), an internationally recognized research and teaching institute on all issues related to disabilities. As Assistant Director of the first HIV/Disability Project, I assumed a management position at the international level. WID is the only international teaching and training center on every type of disability in the world. A master's degree from Penn State and my expertise in chemical dependency made me the top candidate for this particular position.

With the passage of the American with Disabilities Act (ADA), people in treatment with a chemical dependency now fell under the category of having a disability. Also, people who tested HIV positive or were diagnosed with AIDS could receive the same benefits as others with disabilities.

During my first week of employment, I observed a board of directors meeting as part of my training as the newest employee. I was quite surprised that all the voting members were white males! When I later asked my boss how an international institution regarded as highly as WID was governed by all white men, he responded that "black people don't have any money." To say the least, I was very disappointed at this level of institutional racism was still so prevalent. I strongly suggested that every attempt be made to recruit a qualified African American, preferably a woman with a disability, to serve on this Board of Directors. Within the next 12 months this was accomplished.

I began to see that my Caucasian colleagues (peers in terms of having significant disabilities) held very different cultural values and practices. I developed an awareness of what it meant to be a black woman in a culture where people of European decent were more accepted as the norm and started to question my identity in terms of both culture and gender.

My mother had taught me about being a female in the world and in relationships with a man. I loved being a woman, but had never thought much about being a black woman, just a disabled woman. As my awareness of the cultural differences developed, my African Heritage grew more vibrant and my medical diagnosis of having a "severe" (complex is a more appropriate term) disability receded in significance in terms of how I identified and projected myself to the world.

This was a *pivotal* moment in my life. I gained more self-respect and drew upon the wisdom of my African heritage—things my mother had taught me, black art, black actresses, etc. Their greater significance in my life became more identifying than cerebral palsy.

From the foundation my mother laid in my early childhood grew an unwavering self-respect and ability to see myself as an equal to anyone, regardless of income, status or cultural identity. The music and movies I took in, the questions I asked—they had a different focus. Growing up, my heroine

Helen Keller, however, my role models were women of color like Maya Angelou, Cicely Tyson and Della Reese. Even so these role models didn't talk, look like or walk like me. It took 35 years for me to meet another woman with cerebral palsy older than me.

Edith Schneider and her husband were presenting a workshop on sexuality and disability. She held me in her arms and I cried. For the first time I felt a body like mine—one that could not be entirely controlled by the will. Despite the powerful impact of meeting (and feeling) Mrs. Schneider, she still wasn't like me. She just had a body like mine.

When I looked at her, I didn't see myself the way I did when I looked at people of my cultural background. I started to see myself as bicultural— born both disabled and black. This phenomenon is rarely recognized or considered by the medical professionals, educators, speech pathologists and other specialists who work with a wide variety of challenged individuals and their families. Yet, ignoring it means disregarding the values, rituals, or belief systems of the families when designing an educational plan, a rehabilitation program or teaching social skills.

Therefore, the expectations communicated to me as an adolescent, disabled young woman were based on an incorrect frame of reference. Gaining awareness around this allowed me to take control of the decision making process for my life. This change in self-perception seemed to, at times, put me in opposition to the rehabilitation system and other professionals. They saw me as non-compliant, argumentative and uncooperative.

From their point of view, they were correct. Yet, they only had eyesight, while I had vision, persistence and an indelible sense of purpose—a belief in something far greater than society presented to me. I could see, and can still see, beyond the boundaries and what the world initially presents as possible. The African American culture has an oral history and storytelling remains an important way of passing on certain information. This significant cultural difference needs to be incorporated in the teaching of minorities with disabilities.

I have a visual intellect—seeing it in my mind means believing it can happen. For example, when I watched two able-bodied women walk on a treadmill and studied their posture, I knew I could correct my own posture while walking at my speed. Visually, I could penetrate the surface and see what their muscles were doing and then adapt walking on the treadmill at my speed to improve my posture and sense of balance.

I had gone to college and graduate school at Penn State University and except for two years, had lived in Central PA before moving to Boston and then San Francisco. In these multicultural urban environments, I found much more acceptance and integration into the social scene— particularly in the Bay Area, with its "anything goes" mentality, a moderate climate and accessible public transportation. I dated an African American man who used a wheelchair. He was among the "in group" in the disability culture, and people thought we would become the "Black Disabled Couple" of the culture. One huge difference between us, however, was that he saw his disability as his most significant asset, while I viewed education as mine. A presumption exists in the independent living philosophy and in practice that having a disability somehow "qualifies" you to work with others who are disabled. I have always disagreed with this widely held assumption within the disability community.

This change in my identity was most noticeable when I returned to live in State

College in 1994. My previous high academic standing coupled with the work I had done in HIV and disability earned me an invitation to apply for my Ph.D. at my alma mater. Though I hadn't noticed before, now the absence of African American professors in the department presented a significant draw back. In addition, I found the appearance and lack of comprehension of the political aspects of disability unacceptable.

Those who once knew me no longer understood the familiar image before them. What I once viewed as a favor, I now understood to be my legal right.

It was no longer someone else's generosity for which I felt indebted, but rather something I had worked for and was entitled to. I wasn't disrespectful, but now saw myself as an equal. This self-evolution was not readily accepted in my former department. I found little support for my studying the African American disabled population. I chose not to finish my Ph.D. largely due to this lack of appropriate faculty from which I could select a committee. At this point I changed direction in my work and took a job at the Academic Support Center for Student Athletes.

Chapter 5

An International Perspective

At 21 years old, I took my first trip independently to the Matheny School for Children with cerebral palsy in Peapack, New Jersey via train. They evaluated my mobility and made recommendations as to the skills I would need in order to live and work independently. This was well before any laws mandated reasonable accommodations or even the right to public education for the disabled.

After a week of evaluation, they determined that I would need to be able to cross the street by myself and take a few steps without banister. They gave me my first Canadian crutch (the kind with a cuff just below the elbow) which made these two things possible immediately.

Although I feared crossing the street by myself, counting my steps gave me an end point on which to focus. I could also take a few steps without a banister. I never thought I would do these things alone, and they resulted in a level of freedom that I never expected. I liked it and wanted more!

That summer I tested my newfound freedom by taking a bus to Pittsburgh to see the Pirates play. I met a girlfriend who used a wheelchair. While at the game they announced a double header and I stayed another night with a friend in order to see the next game. I had caught the traveling bug and loved going on my own to see different places.

This desire to travel later translated into self-defined mission work. I started taking my greeting card business with me on vacation throughout Pennsylvania and New England, and tried to establish a relationship with a retail business to carry my poetry. This ensured a return trip to restock their supply.

I learned that the most unique thing that I had to offer was HOPE! I could see it in people's faces. Shortly after introducing myself they would sometimes verbalize their wonder by asking, "How did you get here? Who did you come with?" They were astounded that I had come by myself.

By the time I reached graduate school, I wanted to travel outside of the United States. A British friend who attended graduate school at Penn State invited me to visit him in England where he was getting his Ph.D. I took that trip alone, as a vacation during the semester break in May 1984. I stayed with him on the weekends in Milton Keynes, two hours north of London. On Monday mornings he'd put me on the train to Manchester, where I stayed with his girlfriend. She was a graduate student in Manchester, and I stayed with her in her student housing. As I explored the city, I noticed something different from the

United States. Police officers called "bobbies" did not carry guns. The cab drivers, upon learning that I was from the United States, always had a tale to tell to entertain me.

Still I sought a purpose beyond my own enjoyment for my visits to other cultures. I wanted to help, serve and make a difference. Drawing on my Catholic faith, I wanted to serve the poor. I remembered the Bible verses in which Jesus said that in serving the poor we served Him. That opportunity came in 1996 when the Penn State Catholic community planned a mission trip to Haiti to work in the village of Pondiassou, two hours north of Port au Prince.

They put me in the front seat of a pickup truck after the van ride proved too bumpy. We disassembled my scooter and strapped it to the back of the pickup truck with the luggage. When we arrived at our destination, someone put it back together and off I went!

My role was mainly with the children, who loved my scooter, which they called "Machine" (their word for car). They held on everywhere—you could barely see me for all of the children! They fought each other to get on my lap and I had to ask the student translator to tell them, "No fighting or you can't sit on Miss Annie's lap."

One year I gave a talk to the trade classes for men. They wanted to know all about my life—with whom did I live, who took care of me, did I have a husband or children. They did not assume, like many in my own country, that I couldn't have a life like anyone else.
They also asked why I wasn't depressed, which gave me the opportunity to share about my deep faith Christ and the vast role it plays in my life. I talked about Jesus as my close intimate friend. Their eyes grew wide with amazement, and they nodded their heads, trying to understand. They would have kept me for 24 hours, had I not needed to end the discussion to get some

sleep!

At a birthday party for one of the nuns, a Haitian man took my hand as an invitation to dance, and I joined him easily, following his movements. He had no assumption that I could not dance, as most people frequently do. Also, as an elder, (my age was past the life expectancy in that small village), I was treated like royalty.

I traveled to Haiti three times (two years consecutively) returning on a third trip in the fourth year, after learning of their disappointment that I had not come the year before. How sweet to know that they had missed me in my absence.

The first year, under the most striking set of circumstances, a theatre group comprised of formerly homeless Haitian teenage males entertained us. Their performances had raised enough money to buy them a home and also buy a home for children with very complex disabilities, one of whom had cerebral palsy and was part of the theatre group who danced. It moved me so deeply that someone brought him out to meet me after the performance so I could give him a hug. He spoke no English, and I spoke no Creole, so I asked one of the student translators to convey my desire to get to know him. I wanted to know where he lived, and wanted to see it for myself. They granted me permission to take a car and driver along with a student (Matt Osbourne) into the mountains outside of Port au Prince to the home where he lived with children like himself.

I couldn't believe my eyes. The beds and wheelchairs were from a previous time in history, and I thought "but for the grace of God....." They welcomed me and I could see in the children's eyes that they had probably not seen an adult like themselves. I was their race with the same disability, and yet I was walking. I just walked around and touched them. When it was time to leave, I said "au revoir" (goodbye) and one little girl grabbed the three fingers on my right hand and would not let go. I kept shaking my hand to get it loose, and saying "au revoir, au revoir," but her grip and the pleading in her eyes begged me to stay. One of the staff members had to come and loosen her grip because she just didn't want to let me go. I made my way out of sight before bursting into tears, hoping with everything in my heart to return there someday. I haven't made it yet.

As we drove back toward the house where we stayed in Port au Prince, the driver started pumping the brake pedal. Matt asked what was wrong, to which the driver replied "the brakes went out!" Approaching a very steep hill, we pulled over and walked the rest of the way. Though quite a distance for me to walk, with my crutch in my right hand and Matt holding my left hand, we made it down the hill. Some other students saw us coming and came to help. I'll never forget it!

My experiences in Haiti prepared me for a trip to Zimbabwe. In December of 2002, I had become friends with a student athlete from Zimbabwe. He was amazed that I went about the community on my own. He asked, "How can you do things that you shouldn't even be allowed to do?" When I inquired about the lives of people with disabilities in his country, he said that he never saw them in public, and invited me go home with him to learn more.

The people of Zimbabwe considered me not only well educated and articulate, but also physically fit. My friend's upper class family had a maid, a gardener and a guard who patrolled the property. I met several people interested in establishing the first school for children with disabilities and they wanted to know how to obtain funds and find professionals who would volunteer their expertise. I learned about the extensive physical and sexual abuse that regularly occurred in their institution, and was asked to help. It seemed quite daunting that they considered me able to provide the avenues for such extensive consultation. They actually wanted me to stay in Zimbabwe and work with them. I committed to providing guidance, writing (other than direct service) and advising them about where to seek funding, grant writing expertise, etc. Though disappointed, they accepted my decision.

In addition, they asked me to speak at a Sunday morning church service (for which my student athlete friend translated). I spoke about my disability from a Christian perspective, sharing that I view it as more of a blessing than a curse. I felt such deep emotional appreciation for who I was as an American, knowing that my independent lifestyle and the opportunity to work, much less travel, would be impossible in these countries. I returned to my homeland in the sub-zero temperatures of January 2003 feeling more patriotism than ever before. Now I always stand, often with tears in my eyes, during the playing of the National Anthem.

Along with these mission and working trips, I have enjoyed vacations in some of the world's most beautiful places—the Big

Island of Hawaii, the coast of Italy and a pilgrimage to Medjugorje, where many believe the Virgin Mary regularly appeared. I will always treasure these incredible gifts. I continue to take annual vacations to the beach or to sporting events, usually traveling independently. This is possible due to the legal requirements the American with Disabilities Act placed on airlines and hotels.

I follow the rules set forth by this important civil rights legislation that will have its twenty fifth anniversary in July 2015. I also stay at the same hotel chain (the Marriott), whenever possible since they all look alike and give me a base of familiarity—the hotel staffs always remember me! I tend to vacation at the same beach where long-time friends are nearby so I am not actually alone, without some assistance available. Still, family and close friends worry about me. I remind them that I have traveled like this my entire adult life and invite them to join me!

Chapter 6

A Disciplined Life

Many people misunderstand the word discipline, associating it with being rigid or unyielding, yet actually the contrary is true. Discipline means having a predictable pattern or doing an activity on a regular basis. Though it may seem restrictive, discipline actually brings freedom—when we're disciplined to get things done, we create flexibility with the rest of our time.

Daily meditation/prayer and physical exercise are two disciplines that provide regular structure in my adult life. They have given me stability through difficult times and gratitude through celebratory times.

These disciplines often happen at the same

time for me and motivation is never a problem. Exercise is a prayer of thanksgiving or intersession for someone else. If I can turn something into a prayer I *will* do it! Early in my adult life I would also read the Bible and write in my journal each morning.

In the summer of 1979, a friend suggested that I try Hatha yoga. I bought *28 Day Yoga* by Richard Hittleman, and practiced the postures that it described and illustrated. In about 6 weeks the backward bending curve in my torso started to straighten itself. To ensure the positive results wouldn't turn negative, I decided to get a yoga teacher and attended my first class in September 1979 at almost 30 years old.

In the beginning, my muscles' rigidity and spasticity did not allow for much movement. Attempting 1-2 postures completely exhausted me to the point I didn't think I could do it. But my teacher, Theresa—a shy young woman with dark hair and long dark braids down her back—encouraged me, "Today, you can't do this but we don't know about tomorrow." Though I argued that I knew what my body could and couldn't do, she simply replied, "Maybe you can't, but just *allow for the possibility that it might be true*." These few words forever changed the way I look at limitations, obstacles and possibilities.

Within a year I could perform the standing and inverted yoga postures and had quit wearing the orthopedic shoes and short-leg brace that had been my constant companion every day for over twenty years. My body had changed in structure and flexibility. My left ankle, which had once had turned completely over, now merely rotated slightly inward and for the first time I could walk in "normal" shoes. Within a few years I could wear Birkenstock sandals.

These accomplishments required a familiar discipline forged early on because my cerebral palsy demanded it. I became grateful for the times I had to do the same task over, and over and over again. When gratitude replaces resentment, growth happens in new avenues, and new ways of being become possible. I see this as God's grace.

From an early age I had been drawn to the Roman Catholic tradition. My mother's close friend—an African American woman—was Catholic. At about 14 years old I decided to join that church and went to see Father Monte in a nearby Parish. He kept telling me the things I *had* to believe.

I had teachers, doctors and a therapist telling me things I *had* to do and things I would never be able to do. I didn't believe them. So I resisted believing Father Monte too. It took almost a quarter of a century before that early desire to become Roman Catholic came to fruition.

I belonged to a contemplative prayer group that took an annual retreat to a Jesuit retreat house near Philadelphia. During the opening talk of my first retreat the priest said "you can feel comfortable here—this is your Father's house." I began to cry, as it was the first time I experienced being in my father's house. That day I decided to convert to the Roman Catholic tradition and daily mass dominated my prayer life. I was thirty five years old and over time I began to experience God's faithfulness.

Shortly after that retreat, I moved to Boston, Massachusetts where there was a Jesuit retreat house on the rocky coast of the Atlantic Ocean—just a 45-minute drive from my home. It soon became my home-away-from-home as they permitted me to take frequent 8-day retreats. The director of the retreat program, Father Joe F. McHugh, was my first spiritual director. During his youth, Father Joe's mother had died, and he also had a younger brother with a developmental disability. Also like me, he was small and looked younger than his age. These commonalities made it easy for me to confide in him about things I had never shared with anyone. Whatever my previous image of a priest, Father Joe was not it! He sat slouched down in a comfortable chair with one leg thrown over the armrest. I laughed out loud. I told him repeatedly that though Catholic by faith, I would never officially join the church.

In those days, I didn't have much good to say about Catholicism except for the Eucharist. From the very first time I saw the Host in a monstrance I experienced an encounter with the Body and Blood of Jesus, the Jewish man from Nazareth. Now I had a Father I could visualize and a man to love who had loved me first.

Chapter 7

Femininity

Being a girl was hard work! Everything took such a long time. Learning to dress myself and take care of my personal hygiene needs took an unconscionable number of hours. Thankfully, this has <u>not</u> been the case for several decades. Through my mid-twenties, however, the simplest task seemed endless and that was always frustrating.

Still, I was very much aware of being a female. As children, my brother David (just 15 months older than me) and I knew our bodies were different. Up until the time my mother separated us for bathing and dressing, I always asked why I couldn't stand up and pee like my brother. I wanted to do everything like he did. I had a doll collection, but preferred playing with David. We played cowboys or doctor with my baby dolls and this satisfied my curiosity about the differences between boys and girls.

At age 10, mom told David and I (together) about the birds and the bees. She had a separate conversation with me, however, about menstruation. It was 1960, and she gave me a book that she had given to my sisters, who were 17 and 18 years older than me. Mom didn't have any instruction about menstruation when she was a young girl, and I'm sure that lack of knowledge felt unnerving.

She said, "You're going to get bleeding, and it means you can get pregnant."
I said, "You mean blood?"
"Yes," she replied, "and don't tell any boys."

I couldn't imagine not telling my brother,

because I told him everything. She didn't say anything about hormones or a monthly cycle. So, after my mom left I went to tell my brother, "I know something that girls do that boys don't do." I told him that girls bleed once a month and boys don't.

"No they don't," he said.

"Yes they do—Mommy told me."

"Really?" he said.

In this context of superstitions, incorrect language and lack of age appropriate peer relationships, I entered puberty. Though some might say I didn't receive the proper sex education, I found something absolutely wonderful about becoming a woman. Watching my body develop breasts (which happened rather quickly) and seeing curves become a part of this tiny body that I had been learning to control was a fascinating and enjoyable experience. I was physically becoming a young woman, and I loved it!

Many perceive disabled females as girls who will never become sexually active or even have that desire. Nothing could be further from the truth! This misperception of our bodies leaves us more vulnerable to sexual abuse and rape. The unusual curiosity about our sexuality resembles voyeurism—especially among caregivers and, unfortunately, even good physicians. Thus, we are often denied routine pap tests and mammograms considered necessary for early detection of cervical and breast cancer.

Like most girls at that time, I was told that a woman could be a nurse or teacher, but not a doctor or a lawyer. Girls were supposed to aspire to become a wife and mother and that's what I wanted, but I didn't know *how* it would happen. There weren't any images or role models that had bodies like mine or talked like me.

Despite growing up without an adult male in my home, I always imagined having an intimate relationship with a male. After years of fantasy boyfriends, school-girl crushes, and occasional actual dates, I decided I wanted to develop a relationship that would include physical intimacy. I had enough of a positive self-image and body-image to know that some men found me physically attractive. I wasn't confused about sex and intimacy like other young women because I had little experience of men pursuing me as a sexual partner even though I was in my thirties.

As a graduate student in the fall of 1984 I discovered the freedom of dance improvisation. Barbara, a dance teacher in State College, taught me. Her studio had windows on one side and mirrors on the other, so I could watch myself. The soles of my bare feet loved the feel of that hard glistening wood floor. Like swimming pool water, the rhythm of the music held me up, allowing me to move, swirl and glide in the open space uninhibited. It felt so different from walking.

My dance teacher said that watching me move rhythmically across her studio made her feel jealous. That shocked me! Dark-haired, slender and attractive, she had performed and taught dance for many years. She said that moving with such fluidity made me appear graceful and confident, and to her that equaled attractive. She asked me how that was possible when it took so much more effort for me to do everything. I told her that my mother taught to be proud of myself as a woman.

Though Barbara worked with me privately but she always invited me to the class performance at the end of each 10-week session. During the first one I attended, a man in only blue tights holding three silver rings performed a dance that he had choreographed called *The Ring Dance* to music by Fresh Air. Watching him I thought, *before I die I'm going to make love with that man.* Though I didn't even know his name, I believed it would happen, as sure as the sun coming up in the morning.

We had no friends in common and he lived 12 miles outside State College, so I didn't know how it would happen. Then a discussion group about humanistic psychology formed and we both became members. I noticed him looking at me during the first several meetings, but we never spoke. After returning from vacation in Great Britain (May 1984) I attended a meeting at which he overheard a friend welcome me home. Robert (I knew his name by then) asked where I had gone. "England," I replied.

"How did you get there?" he asked.

"On an airplane."

He smiled. "I mean, who did you go with?" His eyebrows raised when I said, "By myself."

During the meeting it came up that I had been writing poetry for 12 years. Instead of asking me what I wrote about, Robert asked me why I wrote. I remember looking directly into his eyes and saying, "People need to eat and breathe. I also need to write." He didn't say anything but I noticed that he kept looking at me off and on until the meeting ended.

As the group said its good-byes, Robert invited me to visit him at his community. As he walked me to the door, he slid his hand along my arm in a gentle caress.

That summer was the end of my graduate school course work. I was taking 6 credits, a 3-credit course and an independent study on death and dying, which I hardly attended. Instead, I spent the summer days sitting in the sun at the nearby community watching Robert go about his daily life—working on cars and cutting wood in the sawmill. Every now and then he would come and see if I needed any water. I always took my lunch and we would chat.

Just as I found it difficult to talk, Robert had difficulty articulating ideas and feelings. We came to know each other through touch, dance, smell, the sound of our laughter and our countless facial expressions.

There was a new baby in the community—Rose. Robert would carry me piggyback up the hill for meals with her parents and 2 year old brother, Joshua. Like me, Robert loved small children and babies. So we frequently took care of little 3 month old Rose.

A strong physical attraction was growing between us, but very slowly. As older adults, we knew it just wasn't time to act on that attraction. Dusk would come and I would say that it was time to go home, and he would drive me into town.

At some point during that summer we took a trip to Maine in Robert's truck. He invited me to go with him when I told him my plans to vacation with a friend who lived on a nearby island. We left late in the day and drove all night. When I got sleepy during the long ride to Maine, I would lay my head in his lap and sleep. I was small enough to fit quite easily across the seat.

Being around Robert was interesting and different. My slowness didn't seem to bother him. He could slow down to my pace as if it were his own. So I never felt rushed with him and he never got in my way with quick movements. He was the first man with whom my disability wasn't a significant barrier to being together for long periods of time. It's not that he didn't notice or that he didn't care, just that it didn't hinder the development of our relationship. My disability created an opportunity for intimacy on a daily basis in a way that doesn't naturally occur in the life of the able-bodied.

Robert most clearly expresses himself through touch and movement, not words. For convenience and to avoid embarrassing messes, I use a cup with a top with a hole and a straw to drink. I'm never without it. Robert would spontaneously take a drink from my cup with the straw which was a gesture of familiarity and comfort that I had never experienced before.

Upon returning from Maine, I visited the community to sit in the sun and read, as my usual habit. That evening when I asked Robert to take me home, he said, "Why don't you stay with me tonight?"

By this time, we knew each other well and I trusted him. He said, "I would like to make love to you, would you like that?" I said "I don't know, I've never done that before." He was extremely surprised that I had not sexual relations before, since I was 34 years old.

His bedroom was a loft so he carried me piggy-back up the ladder to his mattress on the floor of the loft. We made love most weekends for the next two years. Sunlight came through the part of the ceiling that was covered with plastic and we would wake up to see the early morning sun. We enjoyed making love in the early morning.

Sex was like dance—no spasticity, simply fluid movement with another human being during which the involuntary movement that accompanied my cerebral palsy was suspended, as if I had no disability. Normally I needed intense concentration for movements like walking, talking and feeding myself, but not so with sex. It was like a dance—spontaneous, fluid motion. The dance was richer and more expansive in that loft.

A friend noticed a difference in me right away. She told me how wonderful I looked. "What's different? Your hair? Your dress?" she asked. She even caressed my cheek and said that even my skin felt different. Finally I told her that I was involved with a man.

Chapter 8

Interdependence

If I could dispel one pervasive myth in the United States, it would be that of independence. Doing things for yourself, by yourself has its place in human development. We reach true maturity, however, when we recognize interdependence as the healthy way of life.

We need each other in order to live responsibly. Many people ask me if needing help on a regular basis makes me feel bad. It doesn't because we all need help sometimes! Why do we view the "supporting cast" of an emergency room physician, differently than the many personal assistants that help someone with a spinal cord injury? Don't both perform life-sustaining tasks? I'm not suggesting equal pay, as individuals working in an ER have much more education and training along with a much higher level of liability for any errors or misjudgments. The personal assistant's work, however, is often devalued and considered menial. Wage dollar amount isn't the only way to measure the value of certain jobs. Putting personal assistant services under the category of Medicaid suggests that a dollar value can be placed on a person's life-sustaining care which can then be marketed. Therefore, the tasks performed are devalued by giving them a monetary wage.

I grew up years before the Independent Living Movement, which was similar to the Civil Rights Movement of the 1960s. In fact, the American with Disabilities Act (ADA) was similar to the Civil Rights Law that brought some level of racial equality for African Americans. For the ADA legislation, however, the disabled were the target population seeking equal access to public buildings and facilities. Therefore, in order to stay out of an institution, I had to imitate the able-bodied population by performing all the activities of daily living like cooking and eating independently. Group homes didn't exist, so the disabled were either in the world or hidden from public places. Rarely was someone even slightly disabled seen doing regular activities associated with maintaining an independent life; e.g. grocery shopping or going to a bank.

Other than one's family, no assistance was available. I created my own system. The Christian church became my social service system, and I became my own case manager. As an active member of my local church, I let others know my needs as well as the ways I could regularly contribute.

Those who had time simply volunteered to help me. If we weren't already friends, we became friends through our regular interactions as they helped me with housekeeping, laundry, grocery shopping and other errands. The focus became the friendship, not necessarily the chores. Neither of us viewed these times as anything extraordinary, nor could we say that we lived completely on our own. Rather, we needed each other. Receiving assistance promotes greater integration between the able-bodied and disabled populations, and promotes health for all involved. It even impacts those who observe the interaction.

For most of my life I managed to stay outside of the system. I'm not critical of those who choose to use it. But it takes more effort to maintain a sense of dignity and privacy when your life is managed by a bureaucratic agency, especially as a person of color. The people making decisions about the validity of your circumstances to qualify for services oftentimes differ in cultural background, values and beliefs.

Over time I have learned to recognize the different motivations of people who volunteer to assist me and quickly decline the offers of those who wish to make themselves feel better by helping me. A healthier dynamic is simply when another adult recognizes my physical limitations and offers to help. Or when asked to help, bases their yes or no on desire, availability or alignment with their values.

For instance, when a friend retired, she had some extra time and said she would enjoy picking up a few groceries or running errands if I needed it. She did not offer help that required her to spend a lot of time with me, so I probably would not ask her to be a companion on vacation. It is my responsibility to take care of my needs, either by doing it myself, asking a friend or using the social service system. I refuse to be manipulative or apologetic in articulating requests for help, as it shows a lack of respect for others and myself. Self-pity is a luxury I cannot afford, any more than I can afford a Cadillac.
I particularly enjoy when someone of a younger generation assists me. As a mature, adult woman with a complex

physical disability, many people consider it a privilege when I ask them for assistance. Living in a university community, I am afforded many opportunities to influence the perceptions, attitudes and stereotypes towards those with complex disabilities.

One young man, who once traveled as my companion on vacation to the beach, specifically articulated how honored he felt helping me when I was so vulnerable. "I know you can take care of yourself, Annie" he said, "I watch you do it every day. So, I feel very special that you would allow me to help you."

The relationship that evolves out of providing regular assistance for a disabled person is complimentary, and not necessarily "taking care of someone." A reciprocity, mutual respect and intimate friendship can develop over time that is difficult to articulate.

Living Beyond Boundaries

Chapter 9

Athletic Mindset

Though I never wanted to compete in athletics, developing physical strength has always been important to me. Regular weight bearing exercise reduces most of the systemic health problems associated with aging for all of us, including people with cerebral palsy. As early as I can remember, I played and tumbled on the floor. At the very first overnight Easter Seals summer camp I attended they held a circus with disabled campers as acrobats. This is when I learned to concentrate intensely to make my body do what seemed impossible.

This was such a fun way to exercise and stretch my tight muscles! We laughed when we fell and the staff erupted with applause when we kept our balance through a series of acts. I felt like a winner! There were no losers.

I began swimming and horseback riding early in life. Physical therapy felt like treatment, but exercising and staying strong felt FUN and helped me form a positive body image from a young age that remains today.

Between the ages of 14 to 18, I attended Camp Lend-a-Hand, a camp for "crippled" children located near an amusement park. These were the BEST summers as the same group of friends returned year after year. I participated until graduating from high school in 1968.

During college, I became best friends with an elementary school teacher who traveled abroad during the summer. The summer of 1977, we took a cross country hiking/camping trip out west. Another woman joined us for the adventure. In Chicago we stayed with my sister and enjoyed the sights of Chinatown and the Museum of Science and Industry in what remains my favorite US city.

After leaving the "windy city," we stayed in KOA Campgrounds and cooked on a Coleman stove (which I had never heard of before). I remember walking the l-o-n-g incline to Mount Rushmore and hiking the Bad Lands of North Dakota where we saw the Passion Play with live animals and visited the many Native American villages with their exquisite art work and beautiful turquoise jewelry. It was slow going, but my best friend believed I could do anything she could do. "If you tell me how," she'd say, "I will help you." I was a bride's maids in her wedding. The years run together after so much time and so many adventures.

Although I had been a NFL fan since the early 1970's, my passion for college sports developed after I began working for the Morgan Academic Support Center at Penn State University in the mid '90s. Until then, I mistakenly believed that college athletics was a philanthropic gesture on the part of universities. What a rude awakening to learn all the rules and regulations student-athletes had to abide by, let alone booster club members and season ticket holders. I learned a whole new vocabulary along with the rules to basketball, wrestling and soccer.

One might say I have spent too money (mostly gifts) traveling far distances and have even gone out on my electric scooter in icy weather just to see Penn State student athletes play. Whenever student-athletes entered my life, I became their biggest fan. I've had the privilege of attending team practices of several sports, getting to know both coaches and players. I always had my favorites.

One of the greatest privileges of being so close to these young athletes is comforting and encouraging them after an injury, especially a torn ACL which can require 9-12 months to completely recover. Through helping them, I've gained strength and determination to live with courage, fearlessness and dignity. It may sound strange, but watching them fight their way through the tears, pain and disappointment to compete again has been so special. I hold these images of courage and overcoming odds in my mind. Disabled bodies are NOT disabled people. The able-bodied are not "more capable" as people. We are all just PEOPLE! Language, especially the English language, doesn't allow much expression of the many ways we are the *same*.

Chapter 10

The Impact of Loss

Any major life transition—positive or negative—can be defined as a loss. A job promotion as well as unemployment, the birth of a child, divorce or change in disability status for the better or worse—all these changes include a loss of some kind. A loss of a professional identity or social status can be as devastating as the death of a loved one. With the latter, family and friends quickly recognize and assist with the grieving process. But oftentimes we neglect to support those going through other types of loss.

This concept of loss has always been a major part of my life. The first words the doctor spoke over me were that I wasn't breathing and was probably dead. Since age 6, when my father went to work one day and never came home, I've had to deal with loss and the reality that anything material is not permanent. After three months, his body was found in a river.

When I was young, people with developmental disabilities died at a younger age. During my teenage years, three people close to me died—two friends and my favorite teacher (from cancer when I was 17). From 1968 to 1984, every four years someone close to me died. So, one might ask, where does my joy come from in the midst of such profound grief?

The answer to this dilemma came when I worked for two years as a hospice volunteer. Why would I choose to volunteer with patients with a prognosis of just 6 months to live when I had already experienced so much loss in my life? I wanted to know if loss would feel different knowing that their life expectancy was just 6 months from the time I met them.

I learned that time was more about living like it counted than life coming to an end.

Doing hospice work gave me an intimate, close-up look at life and death. I allowed myself to become vulnerable to the patient, sharing what we both believed were the most poignant moments of our lives. A spotlight shown on the significant aspects of living not dying. Little was left to the imagination. Our limited conversations were void of innuendos—everything became clear, crystallized and sometimes filled with humor.

Once I expressed gratitude to a young man that he didn't seem bothered by my disability. He smiled and said, "I'm not going to have to look at it very much longer." We both laughed! Few situations in my life felt as untainted by the false, superficial or somehow disguised. I was learning how to live like each day mattered.

The most exquisite lesson of experiencing many losses over time is discovering that joy and sorrow reside hand-in-hand within the deepest cavity of my heart. Joy and sorrow intermingle, tears and laughter spring from the same source. Sometimes I feel urgency about life, like if I don't do something right now, I'll never get the chance. Or if I leave on vacation, my loved ones will die before I get back. Learning that love transcends physical death has somewhat reduced these anxious moments. I still experience the love of those closest to me, even though they passed on years ago.

Another significant loss in my life was when I quit wearing my orthopedic shoes and short leg brace—a significant part of my identity. The short leg brace was the first identifying information I would tell a volunteer picking me up for a ride. I had worn that support for over 25 years! For 23 of those years, it was the first thing I did in the morning; get dressed and put on that brace with the orthopedic shoe attached. It was one of the most significant things I did at the beginning of each day, because that's what allowed me, I believed, to live life, and to go about my day. So when the progress I had made practicing yoga postures corrected my left hip and aligned it, I no longer required that brace, I had to think of another way to describe myself, another way to answer, "How will I recognize you?" For about a year after I no longer wore the brace, I kept it beside my bed where I could see it. When a friend asked me why I did that, since I didn't need it anymore, tears came to my eyes, I said, "I don't' know, I just want to see it." Shortly after that conversation, I put it in the closet, and in 1986 when I moved to Boston, I threw it away. I buried it.

One of the positive gifts of experiencing such profound loss, which comes as quite a surprise, even to myself, is that grief has caused a deep cavern in my heart that it enhances my appreciation of each individual's life experience and of the human experience. In the midst of such suffering, there are only two choices: to allow your heart to break down or to break open, to become paralyzed by fear or walk through life step by step. I choose to live like it matters, like each day counts.

Chapter 11

My Life's Rhythm

Human beings mature and grow in a variety of ways. From the time of conception, aspects of our being grow, change and develop to make us distinct and unique from anyone else in the world. We also develop our own rhythm of "dancing" in our lives.

As we mature, people recognize us and, on occasion, dance to the same tune or at least a similar one. We call this "connecting" with one another. Living on my own and controlling my environment was perhaps the first such pivotal moment that set the melody by which people would begin to recognize me.

Now, 33 years later, people see me as an independent person who may need a little help, but can take care of myself. Someone who can articulate what help I need and exactly how others can assist me.

Another turning point came when I realized that I could make a contribution to my community—that my presence mattered. People have confided in me since I was a teenager. My special education teacher confided in me about her emotional response to working with children with disabilities. It wasn't all positive, but I remember listening in a way that made her feel better about herself and her job. My non-judgmental ear remains a highly valued gift I offer to friends, acquaintances and sometimes even strangers. I try to remember to ask before offering an opinion.

Usually people end up talking to me after they have been told what they want to hear, rather than given honest feedback. I can be rather harsh, but age has mellowed me a bit. I've tried to soften what I know will be difficult for someone to hear.

My greatest joy is being a respected elder among young people. As I take my scooter around the Penn State campus and even to high school athletic events, I hear young voices shout, "Hi Miss Annie!! Hi Miss Annie!! Are you coming to my game?" "Of course!" I answer back and smile. Coaches and parents alike look for my scooter's flag to see where I'm sitting.

I remain aware of the frequent need for people with disabilities and their families to be given advice or help. Entering a new school system, finding a doctor or a church community can be more challenging with a disabled family member. I make it known that I am available to assist with these transitions in a university community that is ever-growing at an alarming rate.

Growing up at a time when disabled people weren't allowed to do many of the things that I wanted and had the ability to do caused me to develop a thesis about rules early in life. Though not necessarily made to be broken, sometimes rules should be side-stepped in order to negotiate access to opportunities for the disabled that the able-bodied world enjoys.

People say, "If anybody can find a way, Annie can do it," or "it is best to let her figure things out. She's good at finding a creative way to get things done." When I was younger, people interpreted this as uncooperative, or not knowing my place. As I matured, this changed. People saw me as one who could be trusted and counted on as a good advocate.

When legislation passed that allowed more access to education and public life, my rhythm of rebellion took on a more fluid way of communication. I learned to follow the rules and lead those with whom I had argued. They knew the dance better than I did, so like a student is led by a dance instructor, I learned to follow. Whenever possible I chose the people I wanted to follow, like my own doctors.

Acceptance and equality is critical to the disabled. It's not so much knowing your "place" as it's knowing when and how to follow someone who is trying to working in your best interest. Today the disabled along with many other cultural groups do not hold equal political power or equal access to economic opportunity. This is not fair, but in order to bring about change, we must learn to cooperate and negotiate with those we once considered adversaries. Only when all else fails would I recommend considering litigation as such action is, does have a place in establishing more appropriate treatment of those who experience institutional bias based on disability, ethnicity, gender; etc.

All of these strategies allow for the

possibility of interrupting the predicted behavior early enough for positive change to happen. I believe that most people, like doctors and human service workers, just want to do a good job. But given the political structure of most systems (like insurance, individual education plans for the disabled and welfare) their hands are tied. This rigid structure legally limits their ability to be flexible in the way they offer services. This discord makes the "music" off-key, and the dancers become confused in the way they move—out of step if you will.

Behaviors I learned in early childhood have helped determine my rhythm of life. One of these is telling the truth. It's not that I don't ever make deliberately inaccurate statements (we all do that), but I don't intentionally deceive people. I won't tell someone I love them if I don't mean it. If someone tells me they love me and I don't love them back, I respond with "thank you" or don't say anything at all.

Most of the time, it's more important for me to feel trusted than liked. I don't like everyone, so why should everyone like me? As a result, my behavior is not usually predicated on what others think of me. Over the years I've come to realize and appreciate that the able-bodied also feel vulnerable—even fragile. A close friend recently commented that his day wasn't "that bad" compared to something I was going through. I wondered if I had done something that contributed to the way he felt. From my perspective, his experiences were just as worthy of concern as mine and I communicated my availability to help should he need it. Those of us outwardly disabled must not only receive support, but offer it to the people close to us. They need us as much as we need them.

Our personality, attributes and characteristics form ways of being that create a pattern and tapestry by which others fully recognize us. They comprise our social being—who we are in society. Our rhythm of life isn't so much about our behavior, but how we do life in general.

Chapter 12

Crisis in America

The United States is experiencing a healthcare crisis for senior citizens and the chronically disabled. Globally, a significant increase in functional disability among those over the age of 65 is expected in the near future. The aging population and increase in the number of people with chronic health conditions choosing to live in their communities rather than institutions has caused a much greater need for home-based care (non-medical assistance for carrying out routines of daily life like bathing, dressing, cooking, light housekeeping and running errands).

As someone raised with the assumption that I would one day live independently, I learned early in life how to do or request assistance with these types of activities. I know those I can perform and ones like water exercises and others with which I need help. As people offer to help me with laundry and grocery shopping on a regular basis, I recognize the value of what I offer them—a non-judgmental listener and loyal friend. We share common values and they expressed a desire to help only *after* a friendship had formed.

I feel most comfortable asking for assistance within the various churches or faith communities where I've worshipped. The mutual gratitude in being part of each other's lives and experiencing an ongoing friendship outside of the assistance offered and received is beautifully healthy.

Recently, I began a practice of asking a friend to tell me something "ordinary and boring" about his day. When the mundane experiences of others become more exciting than the "highlights" then we get underneath the superficiality where most social interaction takes place. In this space, everyone receives care. It develops its own rhythm as the assistance required by one or more people fits into the pattern of the family, community or church.

Years ago, I attended a talk by Dr. Cornel West, a noted African American Theologian affiliated with Harvard University. I listened closely as he expressed his thought-provoking opinion that America's downfall would be putting a price on something that wasn't marketable. In my opinion and experience, this applies to our current situation with home based care services. Even though this may be the only option to receive the necessary aid, such assistance should not have a price.

I don't have any clear, decisive answers to the dilemmas America faces, but do have some suggestions. As someone who has experienced the three roles of client, provider of care and manager of a program teaching about disability issues, it is imperative that the medical community redefine what constitutes health. It's not a matter of being healthy or unhealthy. Rather, it's a matter of **BALANCE** according to age (chronological and mental) culture and lifestyle. This perspective gives a much broader range to gauging a person's vitality, regardless of any diagnoses they may receive.

I live completely without shame or blaming any person or even a divinity for my life circumstance. I see it as the "hand I was dealt" and have managed to find and create a few jokers in the deck. A daily ritual of prayer/meditation, regular cardiovascular and weight bearing exercise as well as a sense of humor have sustained me through some difficult times and provided unexpected opportunities to celebrate life and share in the joys and sorrows of a caring community in Central Pennsylvania where I have lived most of my adult life. It has become my home when I had given up on ever feeling like I had one.

Investing in one or two intimate friendships over time is of utmost importance. My closest relationships have recently changed with the passing of three of my longest and dearest friends. Grief from multiple losses is by far the most painful thing I endure. The spasticity of cerebral palsy and aching joints from osteoarthritis do not compare to the deaths (some unexpected) of loved ones over the years.

At this writing, I recently attended the final ritual for my brother, a generation older. The familiarity of mourning (the initial stage of grief) grips my heart. I feel immeasurably blessed to find myself able to love again.

To my surprise, I live in Central Pennsylvania where I began living

Independently in the mid 1970's. The political climate, however, has changed and

I face some of the same stereotypes that existed during my undergraduate years. Chronologically, I am a senior citizen or elder (the term I prefer). Elders form intergenerational relationships more easily since they crossed the artificial boundary of time and experience more flexibility than in their earlier years. For example, building and maintaining a career, plus raising a "nuclear family" (a term made up by a sociologist) requires time specific activities that allow for little flexibility, at least in the United States. In other countries, it is common to see couples where one person is much older than the other but the age difference doesn't matter as much because the *extended* family is the unit.

Herein lies the problem with aging and disability in western cultures dominated by western male thought and stereotypes—the arbitrary assignment into stages of life is NOT based on actual lived experience. Little authentic data exists that establishes what is most appropriate as one grows older. For example, I was raised during a time in history when the disabled were expected to walk. It didn't matter how long it took to learn or the number of times I fell. The professional staff who worked with me even taught me to let my body go and not stiffen up when I fell. In fact, I practiced falling!

The focus was to keep trying or practicing. I remember my mother as well as my yoga teacher (decades later) telling me to keep trying and I would get it. They were both correct! I taught myself to type on my sister's manual typewriter and by the time I got my first Smith Corona electric typewriter needed to complete the courses for my high school diploma, I already knew the keyboard as well as the concentrated effort it would take. In a society where success and wellness are measured primarily by linear time and distance, the growing population of elders and disabled will suffer greatly. Since chronological time is a man made concept, it does not consider cultural and individual differences in perception.

There is a dimension "outside of linear time" that those who live in other cultures or practice a spiritual discipline understand that guides their behavior when the clock has less significance.

My mind and body returns easily to the most comfortable routine I ever experienced—the ancient discipline of yoga that I practiced during extended stays in the Himalayan Institute, an ashram located in the Poconos of Pennsylvania.

The ashram schedule:

5:00 a.m.	Rise
5:30 a.m.	Joints & glands exercises; preparation to sit for meditation
6:00 a.m.	Prayers (chanted in sanskrit for 15-20 min) individual meditation
7:15 a.m.	Yoga class
8:15 a.m.	Breakfast

9:00 a.m.	Seva (Sanskrit for offering; this was your job or work)
11:30 a.m.	Prana Yama (breathing exercises)
12:00 p.m.	Lunch - largest meal cooked in the Indian tradition of the Brahaman (highest) caste
1-5:00 p.m.	Seva
5-6:00 p.m.	Free time
6-6:45 p.m.	Light dinner (soup, salad, bread, fruit)
7-8:30p.m.	Evening yoga class (optional)
8:30-10 p.m.	Free time
10:00 p.m.	Evening prayers & meditation
10:30 p.m.	Bed

We kept this schedule six days a week, with Sunday as the "off" day when we usually went to a movie, watched football, got ice cream or had a beer.

In recognition of my slowness in movement and coordination, my schedule underwent some modifications. I worked only half days and rested after lunch. Then a permanent resident (Jeff, a tall young man with a full beard) took me outside for a walk and to play in the snow. Many spiritual traditions, including Christianity, embrace similar practices, and yet it's not as much about religion as discipline that gives us more control over our body and inner experiences.

As you can see significant discrepancies exist between the medical and social service structure and one's *lived experiences* based on ethnicity, life style and religious/spiritual practice. In addition to other countries, the United States has not yet addressed these complex dynamics in providing home based care. The process is just beginning to be addressed, and I encourage you to continue offering your best efforts in bringing about the necessary systematic changes that will allow all of us to live a more balanced, well integrated life.

Our work is just beginning!

— Herald Photo

Dream Comes True—Annie Laurie Harris beamed proudly when she received her diploma during Hickory High School commencement Wednesday evening. This was a special time for she is listed as the first student from Mercer County Crippled Children's School and Clinic to receive a full high school education. Daughter of Mrs. Louis Harris, 122 Fruit Ave., Farrell, and the late John Harris, Annie was born with cerebral palsy. She entered the Crippled Children's School, at that time located at Brady Court, at the age of six Shown congratulating Annie are Jerome Wendel, executive director of the clinic, and Miss Betty Lou Artman, supervisor of special education for Hickory schools.

Living Beyond Boundaries

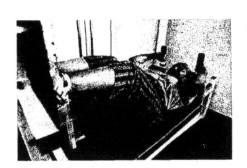

photos by Christopher Weddle

OPENING heavy doors, such as these at the University's Boucke building, is not easy, but Annie Harris can do it by herself and maneuver her electric cart through the door. She travels in the cart because walking is difficult. She has cerebral palsy.

ABOUT THE AUTHOR

Annie Laurie Harris continues to reside near her beloved Alma Mater where she still attends most athletic events. She remains very active by contributing her expertise as a disabilities rights advocate to which her blog "FACING CHALLENGES" (http://annie-facingchallenges.blogspot.com/) is dedicated.
ALL donations via Annie's website goes towards furthering the rights of those most challenged to live in community with the appropriate support as she continues to do.

This inspirational memoir is available where ever books are sold at University Park Campus of the Pennsylvania State University Campus, Amazon.com and by donation via her website.

For more information or to schedule a book signing, email: poetry.cardsusa@gmail.com

Living Beyond Boundaries

38538984R00074

Made in the USA
Charleston, SC
09 February 2015